KINGFISHER FLOWERMAN

Don Kingfisher Campbell

ISBN: 978-81-19228-17-1

First Edition: 2023
Rs. 200/-

Cyberwit.net
HIG 45 Kaushambi Kunj, Kalindipuram
Allahabad - 211011 (U.P.) India
http://www.cyberwit.net
Tel: +(91) 9415091004
E-mail: info@cyberwit.net

Printed at VCORRE PRESS.

Contents

01 > **Surrender**

It was on the Fourth, when my brothers were celebrating the Revolution, that I saw the end. From the sidewalk, our families on lawn chairs in a row watched fountains and flowers explode in the night. Little Shaun held a sparkler for the first time. My son, Jonathan, hands over his ears, just gaped. And I, sitting back, toes in the dirt, my love's arms around my waist, thought I glimpsed the red glow begin. I closed my eyes and imagined never opening them again.

02 > **9/12 Shadow**

I wake up today
and she's gone

The bed is smooth
on her side

Flowers on the nightstand
stand still, unmoved

I walk into the living room,
portraits of Laura remain hung

From my daughter's bed
I'm asked, "Is Mami awake?"

No, Kyla,
I can't tell you where she is

No, I don't brush your hair the same way
but I'll take you to school

There's no one else to kiss goodbye
as I close the door

When I return to the apartment
The TV is off, and I wish I could see

fluffy black hair
leaning back on a couch cushion

03 > **The Margins of Society**

start the poem
in the restroom
of the recently
rebuilt Ralphs

there find
Rest Assured
toilet seat covers
doubling as tissue

and decorating
a few small brown
but very clean
drainage tiles

walk out
the television
camera-ed sliding
glass doors

and lean on
the glittering
faux stone wall
so So. Pasadena

see strewn paper
Rave magazine
one page doodled
by a bus waiter

PUTAS over a picture
of Katia and Marielle
Labeque--Royce Hall
duo pianists

next to the freshly
planted flower bed
three empty
Minute Maid

fruit punch
juice bar wrappers
now sculpture for
an ant's delight

then an Oscar
Mayer / 7-11
Fresh From The Grill
box beside tiny white

planter flowers
by a carefully retopped
Premium POPOV Vodka
Unbreakable Bottle

pointing to plants
that look like
weeping hair
over rocky dirt

free of the market
loose and torn
Twix and M&M
wrappers in the lot

strips of computer
papers and cigarette
butts across from
the loading dock

Milky Way
Big Gulp
and I nervously
peel my

$1.29
Cara Cara
orange
and throw

the peels into
the stone-wrapped
chained metal
trash can

where I can't help
but notice a pile
of men's shirts and
pants lie dumped

04 > **Knowing**

I smile when I want to close my eyes
I hang around while I wish to be alone
I look at buildings instead of wildflowers
This is my daily dolor
I desire to get away from
I have to enter my car
And drive drive drive
So I can find myself
Walking a trail
Feel the crunch of rocks under my shoes
Hear the crunch of rocks under my shoes
See the wind make flowers dance
I walk a way a while
Then I must return
Ask myself why
I leave the earth I love
For another week of structure and structures
I madly learn to
Pay the bills
Come up with rent
I buy music and write poetry
That I may someday really remember
To forget the material
Rejoin the planet
But I'm not ready
For such advancement yet
The perfect bliss
Of being
A shrub
In the desert

05 > **Micro Cosmos High Lights**

1

through blue sky
and white clouds
land on green planet

2

flowers open
like delicate
red paper

3

each tree
a lone creature
like a man

4

a field of trees
a city
of rooted men

5

a moth so still
it blends into rock
until a breeze

6

is it possible
Lewis Carroll
a clown caterpillar

7

an army
of grass
blades

8

a single grass
blade walked upon
by a caterpillar

9

a caterpillar
like a sock
inching up a twig

10

plant blade
is a highway
for a ladybug

11

hyper antennae of ant
a nervous mother
checking each grub

12

sleeping butterfly on stem
like a flower
sways in the breeze

13

two snails approach
touch slimy antennae
recoil at the pleasure

14

snails undersides match
an undulating embrace
heavy shells slowly pull down

15

orange caterpillar emerges
from clear shell
a fruity gummy worm

16

spider wraps
a grasshopper in silk
like a burrito

17

caterpillar caravan
undulates across plain
like a train

18

caterpillar traffic jam
bunched together they twitch
like a Swiss watch

19

two ants share a water drop
stroke each other with antennae
the whole time

20

an ant lugs
a dandelion stem
like an oversized umbrella

21

wasp nest
looks like a
big bug eye

22

gelatinous grubs
beat like
clear hearts

23

dung beetle back legs
push earthen ball
Sisyphus lives

24

a monstrous bird
shadow pecks at ants
roaming the ground

25

dragonfly airplane
buzzes on floating leaf
ready for takeoff

26

aerial reconnaissance mission
over water and grass
clouds reflected

27

thunder gods rumble
wind rolls through grass
trees pushed around

28

raindrops like bombs to bugs
knocks a ladybug off a leaf
flowers are umbrellas

29

snail gazes at reflection
in small pool
sticks head in to drink

30

a bee mistakes
a flower for a bee
humps then wipes off

31

two beetles wrestle
make the WWE
seem tame

32

caterpillar army
rests on leaf
munches edge away

33

white clouds drift
across blue sky
eventually disappear

06 > **Dog Months**

First party of summer
better be by June

August is the best,
those longest days

A pool is the accessory
for tanning in the sun

Sunbathe yourself to match
the watermelon you'll eat

Grill them steaks,
warm that chair

Hot dogs
and lemonade

Sprinklers on the lawn,
sun visor on your head

Mosquito buzz
around croquet mallets

Play badminton to the smell
of insect spray

Loud as thunderstorms,
lawnmowers roll on

Flowers leap open
as if to scuba dive in blue air

Time to take a volleyball
vacation

After all, why does a lifeguard
wear a swimsuit

Except for the wet suit
getting full of sand

Fishing in the fall,
but for now, windsurfing season

Boating is especially splendid
with iced tea

Miniature golf is easier
than surfing, isn't it

The real question is, campfire
or picnic

Nothing like road trip
hamburgers

Never forget to let your throat
ride the high tide of soda pop

07 > **Joker**

dance into the new year
stare intently into someone's eyes
act like a ski-masked thief
offer her money for new boobs
lounge lizard your way into being
the toy soldier in her teddy bear heart
take her out for sushi
lean into each other at the booth
as if you were posing for a picture
your smile will portray your new wellness
forget liposuction and wrinkle cream
drive off in a van for some tacos
wait for Santa to arrive with your birthday suits
the next morning walk for tea and ice cream
then leave her at the airport
she'll go to her therapist to talk about you
how you used to exercise together
drink black lemonade
whisper dirty words of wisdom
now life is a boot camp
of chocolate eating
next to a dog
(when you used to snuggle like sardines
in your teepee)
she was a gift to you too
her hands on your back
in your new town children will look
awkwardly when you pass
with arms in the air
you've been reduced to open mike nights
bald as a rapper near speakers
while you reminisce about her feeling
your muscles
you lifting her like a dumbbell
someday you will return
in a tie and knotted hair
raining dollar bills
bringing back her laugh
future bedtime stories for your kids
the book of your life

will be a bottle of wine
to be savored like a train
since christmas trees come and go
like youthful partners moments
when you necked in dark places
took the pooch to play fetch
and bared skin burning memories
amidst purple flowers captured
in a green field horizoning
a cellphone blue sky

08 > **Confessor**

(Confession 1)

I have worshipped on my knees
at the altar of physical beauty

in pursuit of
a gorgeous face

great curving figure
too large breasts

Ah Man
wasn't enough

I needed a mind
to share

dinner drinks dancing
candy flowers jewelry

mixtape poetry everything
for the biological imperative

to save the human race
why

(Confession 2)

I could all ready
think with my penis

use my senses
to take

in scent of skin
curly hair moisture

we made the earth
shake bed break

that went a long way
butt still

I wanted a compainion
to trade with

thoughts on the daily
dolor of existence

the impersonalness
of those who don't

find me attractive enough to
look at let alone talk to

(Confession 3)

We were behind
closed doors naked

in the garden of bush
and tree you bore fruit

suckled our creation
your mini you

my turn I felt
less important

you reassured me
I could pay the rent

help create
fulfilling ours

of making hour nest
beautiful

through IKEA
Citicard SUV

we all wore out
clothes over time

our gifts
collect dust

things get old
why

(Confession 4)

Now you watch novelas
while I sleep

slumber while I
get up to go to school

work while I come
home alone

how we find minutes
to fuck each other

our purpose filled
the progeny dates

we curse in dissatisfaction
on this coupled journey

into shared oblivion
our fleeting of fair

with my higher forehead
graying beard newfound belly

shortness of breath
your diet panic attacks

lack of calls male guru
helping you break through

release guilt so we'll be here
for each other

out of loyalty
when our bodies go

eyes teeth ass legs
formerly reproductive organs

hug like hamsters until nothing
but spirit is left

to wave goodbye to
see you soon in space

where we can say hi
want to spend some lives

together again "what a long
strange trip it's been"

09 > **Millions of Years**

Stars shine

Lava flows

Oceans cool

Amoebas form

Fish swim

Plants grow

Cockroaches crawl

Dinosaurs walk

Birds fly

Shrews squeal

Flowers open

Monkeys swing

Then humans pave it

10 > **Sunny Vale**

Morning ball of fire rises
creating light blue sky

Black crow in tree branch caws
to the still high half moon

Air hugs the sides of passersby
whether car or man
on this asphalt river

Sidewalk banks decorated
with green oaks and bonsai bushes

They front each wooden box
where parked metal eggs rest
ready to convey via circular rubber

The small stick-like vertical beings
dressed like the flowers scattered
like ornaments through civilization

11 > **May Day**

sun is strong

birds sing

trees so green

houses stand

I am walking on

a warmed sidewalk

flowers in bloom

waiting for a tongue

12 > **Mythology**

"To such endless impressions
we poets give ourselves absolutely,
making, in silence, omen of mere event,
until the world reflects the deepest needs of the soul."
--From "Omens" by Louise Gluck

O
Jupiter you are
A small hole of light
In a darkening blue sky

Below
In a pond on Earth
Ducks swim, create little waves
Which glimmer like ribbons

Reflect lamplight
As you and the moon shine
With our sun's celestial power
(Are you both her beloved flowers)

Only you
Are much farther
Than our orbiting fragment
Born out of a collision billions of years ago

O
Jupiter tonight you are
More than a twinkling dot
Rising in the darkened indigo sky

People walk by
The pond and look
At ducks waddling up
Easy to enjoy every day

I want to tell them
Cast your eyes high
Gaze at the shining speck
That doesn't seem to move

Yet slowly rises
Like the grand moon
Far away where no
Eyes can see a distant Earth

We're just a pale
Blue point in that night
Dominated by many moons
And nearby sister Saturn's rings

O
My Jupiter you are
The overlooked sight
Unseen by most denizens

Mothers and children
Throw bread crumbs at
The dark comical ducks in
The park by the pond's shore

Don't think to crane
Even at the gibbous moon
Which provides illumination overwhelmed
By sulfur lamps on poles each evening

The faraway planet
Hasn't been this close
Since 1963 and not again
So proximate until 2022

By then I might be
Getting ringed once more
Because I am at the park
Waiting for my lovely visitor

Who appears
In my life every day
And I am thankful to the heavens
That our sun comes up each morning

So I can witness
The moon at dusk
And her eyes and smile
Beside me like stars to a planet

Maybe we will
Revisit this location in
A future close as our current
Earthly rotating observation

Around each other
Present every diurnal
Forging twilight sparks
With circling tongues

O
Jupiter this time you are
The most welcome new guide
In my changing evening sky

13 > **Adam and Eve in Paradise Kiss**

surrounded by
copious trees

rose garden
where many stroll

so they have to
wear pants shirts caps

but the buss is
pure lip press

the phrase Ooh
La La is reborn

back in their cave
the real ecstasy

of nakedness behind
closed blinds

and the insertion of
God's plan for mankind

orgasms like
flowers bloom

a tree falls
releasing

an organic river
teeming with life

(damn condom
blocks a future)

14 > **Eaton Canyon Alien**

lands on trail

plants reach out to graze

little yellow flowers beacon sky

stream babbles message

rocks crunch under weight of visitor

native lizards dart out of way

shrubs with antennae signal air

orange brush is not on fire

haze straddling mountains looks like remnant of crash

striated rock splattered with white blood

15 > **"Breaking Apart the Well-Wrought Object"**
--title of a lecture by Arthur Sze

A boy jumps around placed purple flowers,
but only to hear his sneakers hit concrete.

He is called away. Framed windows reflect
rectangular room fluorescence. Inside, a cough,

along with occasional creaking chair, or
rustled sleeve on plastic arm indicates

there are breathing bodies, minds composing
in earthy space, as unseen freeways roar

in the nearby distance, waves try to overwhelm sand,
sky reaches to heaven, not quite making it.

The same for this planet's solitary life;
because infestations grow on surface, deep

in the core, a small sun waits to be
born, to throw light on inner darkness;

to reveal creation continues to create bowls
to crash and repair; gold filling gaps; evolved art.

San Francisco Bay Area

Soft golden hills
Like undulating carpet
For perched windmills

On Market Street corner
Naked men converse
While passing women smile

Coit Tower—
Biggest dick
In the city

Golden Gate Bridge
Always on its legs
Still red

Avenue of The Giants

You can say the
Tallest tree in the world's
Got lots of friends

Scary roots of
Long fallen tree
Inspiration for Halloween

Lady Bird Johnson Grove

Sun brightens leaves
Of trees to light
Green uplifting

Moss hanging
Over limbs—
Tree beards

Microculture:
Momeraths living on
Fallen trunks

Clumps of leaves
In the treetops—
Eat your broccoli

Fern fan—
Cool air
Flows through

Fern Canyon

Step on pebbles…
And you'll get
Your shoes wet

Walk the plank—
You'll still get
Your shoes wet

On the canyon walls
Hundreds of ferns
Wave hello and goodbye

In between canyon walls
Fallen trees become
Obstacle course

Twisted tree sculpture
A kind of static
Armadillo

Wild trees
Bring out
Wild humans

Crater Lake

Deer casting shadow
On patch of snow,
Kinda stands out

Deer standing
In front of human—
Ears like radar beacons

Lavender flowers
Attract
Orange butterflies

On Oregon mountain
China girl with backwards cap
Looks American

Pine trees watched
Rain water fill
Pumice hole

Layers of green hillside
Frame raging waterfall
Smoothing stones

Stands of trees
On both sides overwhelm
Road ribbon

17 > **Biology, Chemistry, Physics**

When cells bump into each other
When soil is pummeled with raindrops
When flowers open to the sun
When flies swarm shit
When spiders intertwine legs
When a caterpillar walks on a twig and leaf
When fish kiss
When mice rub noses
When newborn wolves huddle and whimper, claws kneading
When monkeys grab and hold on for dear hair
When a baby nuzzles a mammalian protuberance
When kindergarteners play in the same sandbox
When eyes see eyes and blink
When fingers roam soft skin
When elephants interlock trunks
When whales swim side by side, water flows around bodies
When trees touch limbs
When clouds lose moisture
When planets orbit a star
We generate lightning and thunder through existence, until one of us dies

18 > **Love Arboretum**

The stones
of the past
make for
a lovely garden

Like statues
we stand for
feeling to
just let go

The trees
beseech us
to open up
taste the air

Their branches
like fingers
show how to
reach out

Even a fallen log
still sports
lively leaves
for a while

And flowers
can always
sprout from
skinny twigs

Each trunk
is a base
for extension
to the sky

Every pond
reflects light
and life
growing around

Any turtle
willingly swims
between rocks
for food

Ducks and
fish join
in on
the hunt

So much
living bursting
foliage provides
welcome shade

Water falls
down hillsides
bathing earth
in happy mud

The sparkle
when flow
hits surface
and babbles

Grassy lawns
framed by
bountiful growth
under blue

Herbs proliferate
inviting passersby
to inhale
sweet smells

Bamboo poles
gather close
to share
common roots

A single
orange spherical
reverently mimics
the sun

Pink bougainvillea
hang in
an attempt
to copy humans

Who walk
the vast
green park
holding hands

For you
I spread
my pea-
cock feathers

This cactus
proudly erect
all day
and night

19 > **autumn**

arms of trees still
stretch for the sky

wind blows brown
leaves to the ground

bees continue to pollinate
the bottlenecked flowers

yellow and black wings beat
over hundreds of red spires

the dance of life goes on
jumping in the blue air

alone or with friends
we fly with happiness

to reach the beach
where sand meets water

footsteps in the dunes
on the shore of eternity

20 > **Questions from The Broad**

Did you forget to wash the dishes?
Wish a bouquet of shiny flowers was waiting for you upstairs?
Do you like to immerse yourself in comics?
How about other media?
Jackie O, Marilyn Monroe, Cowboy Elvis,
and more wanted men?
Would you find pleasure in saluting an artistic flag?
Lose yourself in blocks of primary colors?
Have you looked into the eyes of a single man?
Did his beard match the hair on his head?
Was his forward stare much like your own?
Have you ever dreamed of having three penises too?
Is the fire burning in your cabin intentional?
Why does a tear fall on your cheek?
Are you worthy of a crown as well?
When you glance in the mirror do you feel like a fake?
Remember when you could peer up at a dining table?
Ever vomited money, suckled the teats of society?
Does your jaw slacken at America in bright lights?
With the shadows of the oppressed including you?
Who doesn't adore a nice bite in the neck?
How long have our heads been hanging upside down?
Why do we construct a god out of darkness,
Missing a hand, featuring only one good eye?
Is a dead fish on newspaper a true sign of our culture?
Do you crouch and ponder the meaning of what lies on the ground?
Would you create a poem for your tombstone?
Prefer it in running signage on the wall of a museum?
Where have you declared out loud your needs in two words or more?
Why does this wig have a hole in it?
Can a brain take in all the peering pupils, pursed lips, toothy grins?
Even once been lined up with friends under a gun?
Etched a message to aliens on beach sand?
Saluted helmeted leaders of history, because they were just actors?
Stand on the shore waiting for a ship to drop anchor?
Or simply think outside in your purple nailed open sandals?
Are you an exhibit walking past the side of a colossal building?

21 > **The People, According to Ralphs**

A best customer gets
free peanut butter,
savings on cereal,
toothpaste, paper towels,
cake, and oatmeal
(don't use them in that order)

Any other internet saavy individual
might have a need for
Nicoderm
Nicorette
king crab ravioli to go with flowers
(Valentine's Day approaching)
a free lobster tail if you like angus steak

baby formula
weight loss aid
Florastor
(interesting tri-positioning)
bladder supports
Swiffer sweep and vac
(another fun coupling)

gift cards for Spa Finder
Rogaine for men or women
blood glucose meter
herbal essence
Infamil
(catchy name)

Fortify
Right Guard
Tampax
Gillette
Tide Pods or Gain Flings
(I feel so free)

Advil
(after buying all that)

Premier protein product
Allegra-D
Covergirl
instant breakfast
(mmm, chocolate)
olive oil
Daily facials
Prilosec
(?)
Venus razor
(ooh, la la)

Pepcid
Lactaid
Imodium
Citrical
Pedia Sure
Abreva
Purina Beyond
Alba Botanica
organic formula
Chef Boyardee
(finally, something long recognizable)

Fixodent
Playtex Sport
Cosequin for dogs
Good Karma yogurt
Vaseline
Hershey's valentines
(Yes!)
American Greetings
(go together)

Home Sense paper towels
Beneful dog food
Dreft
Ocean Spray
Dr. Scholl's
Vet IQ
L'oreal
Pull-Ups
Sundown Naturals adult gummies
Benefiber
Prevacid
Azo
Citrucel
Nasacort
(?)
Tyson
Knorr
Poise
Depends Real Fit

I think you follow the idea,
these Americans must have
many needs and wants

We are one messed-up nation
dispensing so much packaging,
if you believe the advertising

Cat's Pride Fresh and Light Ultimate
Kroger's nicotine replacement gum
Luvsome dry dog food
Absolut
Jameson
Always Discreet underwear
Metamucil Meta Appetite
Svodka
K-Y
Johnson's Baby
Desitin
(a progressive quartet, what the heck,
all of it)

Had enough?
These are just the coupons
on down to $2

22 > **Thirteen Ways of Looking at Poppies**

Poppies! Poppies! Poppies! Poppies!
Blown around by the breeze
Like citizens by politics

If Moses had hiked this hill
He would have said the clusters of
Orange flames were beautiful signs of God

Walk as a tee-shirted giant
In the land of the poppies
Swaying by the passing wind

Open petals take in
The sunny flow of air
Fed the feeling of being alive

Shadows pass over the poppies
Shoes temporarily knock flat the poppies
The poppies bounce back up lifted by the following

A field of orange and yellow and purple
Brings delightful color to the brown hills
The cloudless blue sky

Kneeling amongst the poppies
Get close to pure beauty
Fitting right in

Spotted desert brush
Enhanced by orange and yellow and purple clumps
Such harmony in the variety of colors

The sign says Poppy Festival
April 22nd-23rd but
It's already here

Bearded and unbearded men stroll
Surrounded by poppies
Smiles all around

Buds hang together
Like a group of poppies
Grow to love the company

Outside with the wind dancers
Sashaying to the music of the breezes
Twenty four hours every day

Put anything next to a poppy
And it's livened up
A bouquet of flowers and object

23 > **Blue Ramblers**

There they are standing together
next to the '64 blue Rambler
purchased with deputy sheriff salary

They stand tall and thin as can be
him in slacks and plaid shirt
her capris and floral blouse

in front of a tract home
all brown and concrete drivewayed
Little did they guess

the chrome would disappear
from their greatest generation lives
because entropy rules being

The house got older, as they did,
only here at the age of 39
his cancer wouldn't appear

until five years later
My father would be gone
in a mere 14 more system revolutions

after that third operation ended
with doctors shrugging shoulders
leaving him to shrink to a wisp

My mother simultaneously ballooned
having tripped over a parked bicycle
in the cluttered no car garage

bringing about a sedentary future
where she sits watching shopping
networks and remembers her

beleaguered husband somewhat fondly
except for his late night cable porn
and retirement affair with another survivor

She has finally inherited a piece
of her mother's second marriage
electrical company stock fortune

Now she takes pills to stem arthritis
Also for diabetes and irregular heart
She's in no hurry to join him

in their stacked cemetery grave
down the hill you can see
so many dying flowers from here

24 > **You are one of the flowers too**

It's even easier to acknowledge Veteran's Honor when it is a lush magenta rose as well.

Take a walk to the Rio Samba, see dresses swirling yellow, orange, and pink.

The Gemini, white center opening out to the sun of red outer petals.

Mardi Gras, you know the brilliance of an electric pink dress touched by frayed brown edges.

Belinda's Dream, the face in the softest hint of pinkish cream that has more layers than you'll ever experience again.

A bunch of delicate white rose petals clustered around each other, Pillow Fight! (Radiating suns in the middle of every pillow.)

Scattered white flowers, near pink ones, next to yellow, a Rainbow Knock Out.

Midas Touch is the goldest yellow imaginable; if roses were money....

Royal Amethyst has cornered the market on lavender, such a feast full of flora.

What's left but yellow heavily tinged with pink, Love & Peace, a perfectly shaped rose.

No, look down at this! Small roses blushing to white...just like Passionate Kisses!

The ultimate coupled rose? A Double Delight of sun yellow vortex and bold red ends.

But what makes this garden complete?

The petite beach-tanned cellphone photographer in her white dress artfully filled with black paisleys, sandal-exposed white-out painted toes, her fragrant smiling face framed by an auburn hairfall.

25 > **Rhyming Timing**

My love loves the seagulls
To her they're a double delight
She digs them by the water
Enjoys their reflection in daylight

My love also loves the flowers
Visits gardens just to take photos
With her boyfriend the poet
They laugh at their name logos

Both love the colors of the floral rainbow
There is red like their passion
Yellow like their fearful hearts
That love will leave them in purple fashion

But love should have no fear of all that jazz
When feelings are pure as white
A little sun is inside every flower
And no petal ever took flight

Without the food of love on board
Cool inside feelings don't have to hide
They are as delicious as pastries
Together hearts are beside

And flourish like a fountain of feeling
Sea gulls line up to witness
The jets of feeling fly by
Leaving faces with smiling kisses

The flowers bloom separately
Then become a team in life
The Olympics of love are won
When a man pairs up with a wife

Families are born from this coupling
They endure the tough times
To come out smelling like roses
New fire in their rhymes

26 > **Going North, Going South**

(1) Old Sacramento

There were clouds in the sky of our feelings
Whether to hitch a wagon to each other
Each of us a separate building to be explored
The nearby wharf of our pasts littered
With dangerous pilings of failed relationships
So we took the train to see signs along the way
For a night we found a chimney to live under
And trees flowered around in approval

(2) Downtown Sacramento

Knowing the Jack of Spades was in my pocket
We strolled the capitol and its stable columns
Looking high to the dome supported by arches
Then the unmoving statues and the fixed seal
Elevated our journey to investigate the libraries
Of our souls—and each of us found a bear

(3) Lake Tahoe

Clouds overtake the sky
Like trees cover the land
Mankind's cars infiltrate nature
People ride the green river
Bicycle across each other's lives
Sometimes a boat appears that means
There is a lake to cross today
The bay hides the stones underneath
Down the hill comes the waterfall
Leading to a babbling brook of sounds
A cliff to avoid, stay with the leaves
So soft and green, dock beside them
Watch the ripples of minutes go by

(4) Reno

We decide to walk in a casino
The neon signs warn us like red
And green lights we need to
Read meanings under lamp posts

(5) San Francisco Bay

The tower in the distance
Only leads to more towers

(6) San Francisco

We have to choose
Whether we are actors
Who ignore signs like
Runaway cable cars

(7) Golden Gate Park

We made it this far and now we're exposed roots
A waterfall of tears has become a pool of reflection
One duck has turned into two ducks paddling forward
We follow the pathways to a bench for a rest
Then the map leads the way to the koi and the coins
Buddha laughs as we are dwarfed by pagodas
Towers and zen gardens but most of all flowers
Transform us into herons standing near bamboo

(8) Thornton Beach, First San Jose Reading

From tree lined beaches we reach the black squirrel
And the white bunny through windows we see
The sun shines on stones, flora, and fauna alike
Our eyes whirl at the wise words of poets

(9) Second San Jose Reading

The sound of guitars and people with laptops
We eat snacks and wait for my turn at the mic
The music stand is used by all whether singer
Player, rapper, or lone poet spitting from the page

(10) San Jose Zoo

Are you a goat, will you devour just about anything?
Are you an elephant who never forgets the good and bad?
Are you pretty inside and out like a pink flowered tree?
Are you lazy as a caged leopard lolling in the shade?
Are you a monkey, always needing to move here and there?
Are you a meerkat, looking around, constantly afraid?
Are you a ring tail, keeping track of your victories?
Are you a wallaby, jumping at every chance to dance?
Are you a blue parrot, repeating everything you've heard?
Are you a tortoise, slow to catch on, when life moves on?
Are you a Volkswagen bus, stuck in the passed?
Are you a redwood, steady and patient as it gets?
Are you a crooked house where kids love to play?

(11) San Jose Quilt and Textile Museum

All I want in our lives is balloons
Starbursts in our hearts
A flowering in our eyes
Someday we'll visit the pyramids
Hear birds in trees and feel happy
Look out at lights in night windows
See butterflies flit over fences
Both of us walking around in briefs
To lie beside a palm tree
Feeding each other blueberries
The amoebas inside us ecstatic
Even anemone dance about like streamers

(12) San Jose Institute of Contemporary Art

Life makes my hair blue like wires
Like I'm on a lonely boat
I can only see a fence blocking me
From beloved candle memories
The hull of my body is in the water
I feel wiped out of your frame
Like a tornado hit and left me a brain
Otherwise I'm just a hairball
Seeking a spectrumed existence
Not a pile of spray cans in my mind
Pockmarking my walls with tools
Like using posts and pegs to place
Forgotten heads into boxes

(13) San Jose Museum of Latino Art

In communities we are merely members
Loved ones thought of as just people
Residents of a citizenry full of families
Police don't want to provide us shelter
We are refugees sending postcards
To friends lost inside of poems
Here a refrigerator is a flag
A sign that gallon water jugs
Reflect the vagabond nature
Of tractors beside houses
Red doors to the unknown

(14) Between the museums

When is a red tree near a yellow cage?
When water fountains flow below banners.

(15) San Jose Museum of Art

Words can be like statues
Like strings can become clumps
A beautiful wreckage like icicles
Bloody heads because donkeys kick
Where are our plates in this setting
Do we hang like glass for all to view
Like a compact disc tossed in muddy water
The way rafts look to birds from above
How do we keep our wheels rolling
In the rain of stones thrown at our days
Don't strangle ourselves with cords
Touch the woodgrain of our relationship
The blue light will guide us through
The marshes of our uncertainties
Inside the corridor of moments
We'll stumble upon a pipe in the brush
Cans scattered like flowers
If we only take these fulfilling steps
We'll glide into and out of troubled doors

(16) Café Frescati

So I can read my poems in an Italian Starbucks

(17) Hakone Gardens

The pools of your eyes are where
The fish swims under the fall
My panes overwhelmed by overgrowth
Our limbs amongst leaves
Clear like a pole in the sunlight
Yet we question the green
Swim in the raked sand
Think a wall is a passageway
If we could simply circle around a pipe
Our hallways might be filled with garlands
Imagine the views of our future

(18) Sunnyvale Community Center

We've seen the fountains and flowers
Gazed open mouthed at ducks and benches
Marveled at an orange tree next to a blue lake
We didn't jump in and swim
Balked at the frothy swirls
Which grew to reflect our gushing
We've paddled from boy to girl and girl to boy
Relaxed in the shade from the sun
The shadows of an unseen family
Posing for a group photo without knowing
The dance steps to totem spraying
A plaque dedicated for flowers and succulents

(19) Ellaraine's Living Room

Six kinds of dark chocolate
As many wines in red and white
Our laptops flashing poetry

(20) Solvang

Finally the windmill trip is about over
We've craned our necks at so many things
A clock on high silently tells we've poured
Ourselves into time, its signposts
Something to watch gallop away
Like an emotional horse in a square stanza

27 > **Trumped**

in a world full of flowers
where you can cherish your purpose in life

he does

and his birds sing along
wishing for a merry christmas

they do

if only we had three wise kings
leading us to the light of enlightenment

we don't

instead there is a big orange bear
who looks at our wallets
with eyes filled with wonder at the beauty
of the profits the world has to offer

until they're gone

28 > **Ohtsu**

I thought I saw
a pile of penguins
bleeding in snow
but no
it was a camellia
flower pouring red
petals on a blanket
its yellow pistol
a dying sun
on a crimson ground
surrounded by flakes
piling up over rocks
and an empty picnic table

where have the people
gone?
they are sensible
not attracted to cold
death by freezing
this disexistence
does not appeal to them
so they are safe
somewhere else
looking out windows
at the white world
slowly burying color
until spring brings
back the recreation
of happy faces
jumping over stones
rolling on grass
plucking flowers from trees
to give to loved ones
while we're breathing
and sweating in the
warmth of it all
seasonally removed
from the danger
of ice falling from
the heavens, oh god
what have we done
to deserve these changes?

that's just the order
of the great
cycle that generates
new life to replace
old weather-beaten
stems of history
turn them into mulch
for babies who grow
into food for predators
who do not go through
unscathed thanks
to the humans capable
of destroying
any creation

29 > **Where in the world**

Can you live in a big city
Eat food from another culture
Tell time analog or digital
Enjoy the flowers summertime bloom
Wonder what is behind window shades
Children in some rooms draw self-portraits
Adults write their stories under fluorescent lights
Hoping someone will want to hear them
Step behind a microphone and hold it
Words slake thirst like water from a bottle
Applause is the cake you eat with your mind

30 > **Nature can't be a hologram...**

trees sway
to the dance
of the wind

flowers smile
hello all
day long

streams tell
stories for
so many ears

lakes like
to contemplate
life and death

mountains sing
their usually
silent songs

rocks are
experts at
lengthy rest

insects, animals
and humans
navigate between

this until
they die and
become recycled

31 > **electricity**

we are side by side naked
in our California pajamas

then we touch fingers to
fingers and toes to toes

our eyes open unlock each
other's awakened hearts

you slurp me into ready
for action attentiveness

I have to slowly enter
your moist charged body

gradually increasing speed
as a fleshy mushroom piston

wanting to go 88 miles per
hour to achieve time travel

seconds into the wet future
flowers explode in my head

a small geyser erupts from
my stilled encased penis

endorphins play around
the front of my sweaty mind

I can feel the factory tubes
manufacture more sperm

as I drive my woman to work
she massages my sticky thigh

and says you're my baby
maker my powerful honey

my hairs stand up a little
with her evocating voice

32 > **Arboretum: 24 ways of looking at bushes, plants, and trees**

Purple fronds like barbed wires
or caterpillars

Trees on fire with no flames

Cactus, the inspiration for Disney Hall

The fern monster emerging from fern lake

Bird of paradise, pointed bill, pointed crown

Tree limbs like smoking log firework

Red and orange and yellow and pink and white and blue flowers burst on bushes
like mid-air firework explosions

The hair of the willow

Branches reach up like arms

Knotholes like breasts

Desert cactus tree crawling with snakes

Desert plant sprouts sea cucumbers

White bell flowers like popcorn

Cat tails, long quills

The fur coat of the palm tree

Forked tree

Bush leaves the color of an amphibian's back

Arcing pink flowers like prawns or shrimp

Cat tail firework burst

Divining rod tree stretches across road

Tree shadows, humans who can't walk away

Bamboo trees cluster, stick army

Cell phone tower, imitation tree

33 > **Simile Love**

1

I love you
like a donut
needs someone
to eat around
their hole

I love you
in the same way
a squirrel has
the ability to
hide their nuts

I love you
as the flowers
use their pistils
to attract
hungry bees

I love you
with my eyes
even though
I have to wear
glasses every day

I love you
by embracing
your body
as if it were
a statue of romance

I love you
like a key
wants desperately
to be inserted
and turn tumblers

2

My love for you
can be a lot
like a lot
filled with cars
reflecting sun

My love for you
claws carpet
thinking it's a cat
sleeping all day
dreaming of tongues

My love for you
charges like a cell
phone connected
to a wall outlet
giving electricity

My love for you
is comparable
to some body
who can't swim
flailing arms

My love for you
would be fine
if it were plastic
and nor degradable
for 50,000 years

My love for you
breathes oxygen
converting molecules
to carbon dioxide
exhalations of passion

3

Love me like
a sandal
slips on
a foot
each morning

Love me like
raindrops fall
onto concrete
leaving an impression
of permanence
evaporating

Love me like
a water hose
left on a lawn
to soak the soil
and stir shoots

Love me like
a dog pants
to release heat
in the sweltering
afternoon hours

Love me like
a clock clicks
signaling seconds
passing forever
in the continuum

Love me like
the frosting
of a cake
makes it all
taste good

34 > **Granada Park Love**

My life has been a series of trees planted in soil
One has purple flowers now
Amidst the abandoned Stonehenge picnic area of my past
Columns rise but there is no roof, no shelter
A tall tree has found its hugger
A lone lamp in a green field
The only pathway surrounded by other arranged arbors
Sun shines on their leaves
An old crown, a monument to age
Young sprouts admire the view upward
She stands waiting to be photographed
Laughs because a bench to rest upon has been discovered
White wisps in the sky signal fleeting time
Light fills dark structures
Trash can tagged and documented
Flowers ignite red, orange, lavender, and magenta
The blue welkin is streaked with feeling
Palms reach for each other
Yellow beacons spark home
Distant city lives its own lives
A single trunk tries to tell its story
Scattered needles on the ground
A belt of sunlight turns the evening
As a plane splits through the void
The Cube has brought us here reflecting hues
Branches lose color in the night
Yet there is a smile on my face
Next to the dear honey of this day's glaze

35 > **At The Broad Museum**

You can find me around the parade of skulls

The building I'm in is firelit even though I can't feel it

She is a sleek modern façade of color

Having arrived for the bright lights of America

I present her beside metallic flowers

Show her she is a very special person

I hope she's happy like a small child under a table

36 > **Fireworks**

a street tree
exploding with magenta
flowers, each like a fourth
of July fireball in August
spiraling out of the green
held up by brown trunk
on the smooth grass
of a traffic meridian
--and look--there's
another one on
a different island
and again, over here
boom boom boom
bloom bloom bloom

37 > **The Music of the Day**

She sits on a black bench
looking cautiously at the world
outside the wooden door

Red flowers spread out
from branches of a tree
above a roof overlooking
verdant canyon below

A boy on stoop steps
toots a flute as a cat
inquisitively wonders

The woman in the blue dress
on a chair thinks eyes askance
as white lilies bloom in sunlight

Two men legs akimbo under
palm fronds discuss
the zither music of the day

38 > **After the Orgasm Starts**

a thick almost clear liquid
emerges from fleshy hole

and flows down to land
in a thicket of wiry hairs

that's because it wasn't inserted
into any unavailable orifice

instead fragrant mess is wiped
with a white tissue that becomes

buttery-colored in the middle
like a wadded vagina and when

this is placed close to the nose
it smells like fresh-cut flowers

if you could bottle a perfume
like this call it Semenal Bliss

39 > **A Street in Haikou**

my love records
from her cellphone
a 15 second video
and pushes send

a blue shirted florist
sitting on a lime
green plastic stool

arranges his
just watered
plants for sale
on the sidewalk

where an orange
bucket sits full
of grouped flowers

his parked van
with an open
rear hatch fronts
a row of curbside
motorcycles

one cyclist
on this sunny palm
tree lined avenue

wears a yellow helmet
and sky blue soccer shirt
as he buzzes past

a multi-story tower
of residences
in the background

the unsurprising
power pole strings
overhead in a clear sky

cars, SUV's, and vans
line the parking lot
of this mini-mall
where leaves catch sun

and green framed open
double glass doors
lead to a faux
marble tiled floor

a potted elephant
eared plant and a
waiting green desk

sports a bright
orange tray and
an empty black
high backed
swivel chair

under a row of
ceiling hung
cone shaped
white spotlights

her friend with a blue
mask on her chin and
fake fire and smoke dress

crouches over a printed
paper while a young short
cropped black haired man
looks across at her as

she signs the mortgage form
on a round glass table
with a wicker base

my fiancée is outside
waiting to walk with her
to the bus stop where
they travel through traffic
to blaring pop music

could be Long Beach
if I didn't know she is
7000 miles away as we

wait for two governments
to agree on when she
can safely return to me

40 > **You are my goddess**

I worship you amongst the flowers
As we hug amidst verdant trees

In the pools of your eyes
The nearby waterfall is your hair

Lipstick sun shines on your lips
Delicate fingers excuse exposure

Your toothy smile is a fortress for happiness
You stick out your tongue for love

The mist wishes your presence
You are my sensuous Mona Mina

How you give a room curves
Lace frames your soft smoothness

Your bra works extra hard for you
You playfully pout to melt this heart

Tilt your head to acknowledge cleavage
Hills or mountains, either analogy creates saliva

Leaves long to enhance their loveliness near you
When you lie down you are a garden

Vertical stripes of my shirt contrast your body so well
Rembrandt wanted to showcase your curvature in the dark

You laugh when I say you're lovely skin glows
Posture in profile, your figure opens my mouth

Blouses desire to highlight your pendulousness
Pull up your shirt, you overload my senses

You make robes want to encircle and caress you
Bras wish to fall off to demonstrate your gifted swells

You are an angel unhooking your brassiere
Your breasts are two eyes above a bearded smiling face

Furniture looks better in your presence
Carvings and curvings play alongside each other

Shadows linger just to grace your symmetry
The air circulates around you electrified

Even glasses cannot hide your sensual stare
From below you are a fifty-foot woman

You are the sexiest ghost in a dark hallway
Mounds is not a candy bar when you are seen, or is it?

You point the way to satisfaction with two points
Nipples in perfect proportion to areolas

You are Venus when you stand naked in a room
Your silhouette turns any window into art

With high heels you become a mud flap
The countryside tries to envelop your statuesque stature

When you recline the joy is in your cheeks
Your gaze combats your pensive thoughts

You lean your head back and ecstasy joins you
You bring the magic out of a clothes cabinet

Pose by stained glass, you are a flame flickering
Your reflections fight for attention with your real gorgeousness

Open a bathroom door, it welcomes your beauty
Erect like a breathing statue under the shower head

Your wicked grin invites me in to pleasure
You act surprised when I notice your pussy hair is a heart

Your legs are long uninterrupted paths of perfection
Toes tantalizingly tickle in nail polished rows

Your fingers spread open Eden for occupancy
A pink bud created for creation, or merely for fun

You slurp my fleshy pole into action
We embrace afterwards to hold on to feeling

41 > **Catzen**

Ah to live the life of a cat

That's where it's at

Lie in a space for hours

Eyes closed dreaming of flowers

Paws akimbo to the empty air

Imagine floating effortlessly

In the happy void there

42 > **2021 Houseless**

A row of motorhomes
with flat tires

Parked by the curb
of a freeway entrance

Motorcycle ready nearby
makes something of a life

Stationed beside trees'
pretty pink flowers

43 > **Is everything art?**

(Inspired by the Getty Center, Los Angeles)

People walk surrounded by buildings

Geometries of the structures themselves

View of distant freeway from lush green hillside

Stand masked in a room decorated with furniture 200 years old

A painting of edifices no longer in existence while children play around a wooden cart in the foreground

Boats float in a canal each driven by an oarsman

A placed stone is a walrus before a pool

The Vision of St. Bruno, cherubs in the sky

Birds with outstretched wings fly away from a waterfall while goats bask in the spray

A tree whose branches and leaves feel as if you could touch them as you walk the dirt path

The strangeness of a bronze sphinx with lion legs and eagle wings casts a shadow on the marble base

A couple dances in the gallery

Blue irises grow on the wall

Succulents whirl outside in a planter

Bare branches rise in a garden row

Pomegranates hang like Christmas ornaments

Man-made trunks bundled into bouquets of flowers

A sculpture empty mouth screams

The prettiest flower in the place is you

(You're my Venus with arms baby every day)

44 > **Sonnet of Aubade, Plussix**

Once more I sniff your skin and am inspired to
capture this compulsion to cross our legs together

I am tonguing my feelings down your throat
because I am watering flowers in our hearts

Easy for me to do since I have a field on my chest
that felt your fingers traipse downward again

My trunk is solid with lifelong memory of attempts
to cultivate love to thrive in steamed moments

When all I needed was to let your eyes swim in
mine far enough to create mutual garden growth

Wherein we play adulthood games while watching
our favorite features of each other's countenances

Yours are freckles on a youthful face smiling
having unearthed a beard being a happy location

It is pleasant to find we prefer penetration in order
to share thoughts become quivering liquid desires

May this journey into discoveries never end only
multiply like days spent beside in posted repose

Walk with me every way we can hold hands as
four limbed creations wishing long entwinement

45 > **The Fucking Museum**

The fucking cell phones
The fucking drones

The fucking death
The fucking war

The fucking gas prices
The fucking food prices

The fucking home prices
The fucking rent

The fucking debt
The fucking banks

The fucking inflation
The fucking greed

The fucking wages
The fucking shopping

The fucking classism
The fucking racism

The fucking jealousies
The fucking pettiness

The fucking pretentiousness
The fucking SUV's

The fucking speeders
The fucking assholes

The fucking cooking
The fucking eating

The fucking shitting
The fucking universe

The fucking relationships
The fucking frenemies

The fucking poetry
The fucking in our bed

That is fucking all that
Fucking matters to me

Oh, and clouds and flowers
And music and movies

Did I already mention
Poems are cheap therapy

46 > **It's All Too Much**

A universe littered with galaxies beyond my imagination

Every spiral stretching outward festooned of stars

Each sun sporting some planets, moons and asteroids

This sphere always covered by untold clouds

Oceans alive since evolution evolved here

Thousands upon thousands of fish, sharks, and whales cruising currents

Shores infested in the billions because trees grow and humans manifest

Beings briefly bringing forth into being millions of buildings and books

Made merrier making music and art and children

A ground even more populated around a quadrillion animals and insects

Enough food and flowers to delight all those eyes and noses and mouths

Burgeoning brains recreate creating electric visions and revisions

I'm just a pixel in a pixel in a pixel in a pixel

Part of the whole shebang breathing in and out

Cosmic light went on, someday I am shut off

To be recycled as the planet pleases until it ceases

Also repurposed multiversally for unknowable time

Does God have a new design planned in the possibly etch-a-sketch future

47 > **No Seals in Seal Beach**

Drove our landlord and her husband
to the Long Beach cruise drop off

Then didn't want to just drive home so
I skirted coastal highway neighborhoods

To the familiar romantic pier where we
always stroll hand-in-hand and look out

At the Pacific Ocean rippling blue,
take cellphone photos of gliding seagulls,

And white wave breaks, palm trees
standing tall in the sun and wind

Walk by our favorite shops to capture
overpriced trinkets and potted flowers

Buy the Surfer's Special, two burritos and a soda
which we leisurely down on a sea-facing bench

With a bag of copious tostadas to later munch
back home for lunch before open door sex

48 > **UNO Party!**

The muffins in the clear plastic
case on the dining table look
like butter and chocolate flowers

The cards my wife deals out
are red, yellow, green, and blue
like rectangular flowers

I gaze up at three birthday balloons
still tethered to the curio stand
naturally bunched like flowers

I turn to the open blind window
notice buds that will become lemons
sway because they are flowers

And my spouse is my favorite
flower to water, thinking this as
she sits and wins, munches and wins

I'm distracted, inspired to poetry,
so I lose the round like a wilted flower,
but gain a freshly budded poem